OLD FRIEND, WE M

MW00713876

OLD FRIEND, WE MADE THIS FOR YOU

Yannick Marshall and Yemi Aganga

FOREWORD BY GEORGE ELLIOTT CLARKE

Kellom Books
AN IMPRINT OF CANADIAN SCHOLARS' PRESS INC.   ◆   TORONTO

Old Friend, We Made This for You
Yannick Marshall and Yemi Aganga

First published in 2007 by
Kellom Books, an imprint of Canadian Scholars' Press Inc.
180 Bloor Street West, Suite 801
Toronto, Ontario
M5S 2V6

www.cpsi.org

"Bass Wilson farmhand" was previously published in the journal *English in Africa*; "Kingston Light" and "Sonnet for my crack princess" were previously published in Ishmael Reed's *Konch Magazine* (www.ishmaelreedpub.com); "Liberation," "Bayakou," "The sojourners," and "The art of poison" were previously published in *Wasafiri* 46 (Winter 2005): 17–19; "All the time in the ghetto, Violence," "Sinai," "Mosquito-net rhapsody," "Bagga ballad," "Procession to dilapidations," "Sea crabs," and "Ndoko" were previously published in *Kola Magazine* (March 2005).

Every reasonable effort has been made to identify copyright holders. Canadian Scholars' Press would be pleased to have any errors or omissions brought to its attention.

Canadian Scholars' Press gratefully acknowledges financial support for our publishing activities from the Ontario Arts Council, the Canada Council for the Arts, the Government of Canada through the Book Publishing Industry Development Program (BPIDP), and the Government of Ontario through the Ontario Book Publishing Tax Credit Program.

Library and Archives Canada Cataloguing in Publication

Marshall, Yannick, 1984-
    Old friend, we made this for you / Yannick Marshall and Yemi Aganga ; foreword by George Elliott Clarke.
Poems.
ISBN 978-1-55130-331-4
    1. Canadian poetry (English) — Black authors. 2. South African poetry (English) — Black authors. 3. Canadian poetry (English) — 21st century. 4. South African poetry (English) — 21st century. I. Aganga, Yemi, 1983- II. Title.
PN6109.7.M37 2007   C811'.6080896   C2007-902615-X

Cover, interior design and composition: George Kirkpatrick

07   08   09   10   11   5   4   3   2   1

Printed and bound in Canada by Marquis Book Printing Inc.

TABLE OF CONTENTS

All poems are written by Yannick Marshall, with the exception of "Mountain kingdom pastoral," "peephole," "Say goodbye to the beautiful voices," and "Bass Wilson farmhand," written by Yemi Aganga. "I write what I like" is also written by Yemi Aganga.

FOREWORD: DIASPORIC DIAMONDS

By George Elliott Clarke

BY BILLING HIMSELF AS "The Greatest," Muhammad Ali staged a one-man (Black) Cultural Revolution. Before him, any honorific superlative attached to a person of African heritage indicated that he or she was *merely* the best, the most..., the finest, *inside* a racial category understood as peopled by natural inferiors. To say, for instance, as did the *Toronto Star* newspaper in 2006, that Denzel Washington is "arguably the top black actor of his generation," is to attempt to discount his superior ability and stellar achievement. Why not state, simply, truthfully, that Washington is "The Greatest" actor (or, if humility is desired, "one of the best actors") of our time? Ali challenged such backhanded compliments: he wasn't just a supreme black pugilist, or the deftest black boxer of his era. No, he was, radically, "The Greatest": Period.

I begin as I do because I must name *Old Friend, We Made This for You* the most remarkable Canadian poetry debut of the 21st century, although only one of its excellent poets—Yannick Marshall—is Canadian. To the English-Canadian Poets Club, so absurdly bloodless, colourless, passionless, lifeless, and rhythmless (and practically wordless, given its choking articulation of anything halfway meaningful), Marshall, with the redoubtable assistance of Nigerian writer Yemi Aganga, delivers the polar goods: the red of tuberculosis patients' blood, the ebony nights of ivory stars and copper skin, the shouts and moans of witness (and hunger and erotic pleasure and, yes, dying), the explosive music of nightclub, shebeen, church, and disco, plus poetry that is dynamic, breathtaking, soul-shaking, and unabashedly brilliant. Yessum, these poets "bring da noise."[1]

How do they do this? Why are they so damn good? Nicely, they explain their miraculous poetics: Following the order of the slain South African anti-*apartheid* martyr Steve Biko, they "write what they like."

But there's more involved than just living up to Biko's insurgent example. Much more.

Marshall is the first Canadian poet to seize hold of all the vast poetic resources of the African Diaspora, and Aganga ably helps him along. Together, they repeat the myth-making of Nigerian playwright-poet and Nobel Laureate Wole Soyinka; they practise the songwriting of Ugandan poet Okot p'Bitek; they recycle the earthy, Africa-rooted imagery of Afro-Yankee poet Henry Dumas (plus the biblical wail of Canada's Frederick Ward); they sound the pungent analyses of Sierra Leone poets Lemuel Johnson and Syl Cheney-Coker; they echo the reggae-based critique of Ghanaian-Jamaican Kwame Dawes; they voice the plangent psychiatry of Martiniquan *philosophe* Frantz Fanon; they even seem to echo Black Nova Scotia's very own and splendid bard David Woods (born,

---

1. *Introduction to the Introduction to Wang Wei* (2000), a verse collection authored by the Pain Not Bread collective (Roo Borson, Kim Maltman, and Andy Patton), re-introduced Anglo-Canucks to the socially conscious song structures of classical Chinese poetry, thus revolutionizing the praxis of *real* poets. *Old Friend, We Made This for You* will educate all those interested in progressive poetics in how to incorporate Africanist, expressive techniques.

appropriately, in Trinidad). (Attention: No Canadian ignorant of these names will author good poetry.)

Crucially, Aganga and Marshall know all they talk bout. They've lived in Africa and the West Indies; they've hung out in Lesotho bars and they've eyed cranky, T-Dot (Toronto) cops.

The coruscating glory of *Old Friend, We Made This for You* is that Aganga and Marshall fashion radical poetry out of the whole, provocative reality of the African world—from a hurricane messing with Grenada to a sermon addressing Nova Scotian (Africadian) history, from starvation in one nation to AIDS deaths in another. They do not shy from pain; they do not run from beauty. They are diasporic diamonds.

These poets are fearlessly wise and alertly mindful. Every one of their lines satisfies the First Commandment of *Verse*—to be song.

Old Friend, We Made This for You is the most exciting and accomplished book of *mainly* Canadian poetry you will read (and *feel*) for years. It is an annunciation of genius. It is Revelationist Poetry. It is exemplary. It is a triumph. It is "The Greatest" debut of our era.

Reader, praise! Poet, kneel!

George Elliott Clarke, O.N.S.
E.J. Pratt Professor of Canadian Literature
University of Toronto
Laureate, 2001 Governor General's Literary Award for Poetry

I WRITE WHAT I LIKE

"The most potent weapon in the hands of the oppressor is the mind
of the oppressed."

—Speech by Steve Bantu Biko, Cape Town, 1971

I am not the right person to write this—this book, this essay. That is
what I originally thought: I thought that my life, or rather elements
of my life and the malignant impression that it was not my place to
voice myself on matters of ethnicity and Afro-centricity, prevented
me from contending with issues of such importance.

And I was oh so wrong.

In the words of Steve Biko: "It becomes more necessary to see the
truth as it is if you realize that the only vehicle for change are these
people who have lost their personality. The first step therefore is
to make the black man come to himself; to pump life back into his
empty shell; to infuse him with pride and dignity, to remind him
of his complicity in the crime of allowing himself to be misused
and therefore letting evil reign supreme in the country of his birth."
Frank Talk.

I watch brothers, sisters, die every day of AIDS, curable diseases
in unstable societies low in democracy, high in raw wealth, while
rich Western governments pat themselves on the back for applying

a cotton swab to gushing rivers of blood that they in part created. And yes it is true, we too oppress ourselves.

And why?

Every day I watch. Every day I watch black Africans reject each other on tribal and geographical grounds; artificial national distinctions dub me "ma kwere kwere"—foreigner. Every day. Every day, I watch.

Every day I watch crime escalate in our societies while social structures disintegrate. Every day I watch African Americans reject African Americans, Africans reject Afrikans of the Americas, both ironically pandering for the affection of the middle class and white.

I reject not the dream of Martin Luther King of little black boys and little black girls holding hands with little white boys and little white girls, but never, never, at the expense of little black boys holding hands with little black girls. Never. Why? Why the Coca-Cola culture?

To borrow a metaphor from Malcolm X, imagine you are coffee, black. Keep adding cream—the more you add the more the taste changes, till eventually you cannot even tell that you were originally coffee.

Why? Why the Coca-Cola culture? Why must I lose, prostrate myself? Why must you, why must we lose and prostrate ourselves before the altar of our own degradation?

And so perhaps that is why we wrote this—this essay, this book. We wrote it for Afrika. I mean Afrika not only the beautiful continent in the geographical sense, empty and hallow in the way some bludgeon her head against the concrete, but in much wider currency. I extend my palms from the continent to the Diaspora, to Africans of the Caribbean, to Africans of the Americas.

It's like Femi Kuti says, I suppose: "BLACK MAN! Don't forget your culture!"

Wole Soyinka: "The move back to Africa by the Brothers from the Diaspora is in itself, without any question, a valid desire. By move, of course, I do not really mean the physical move, although this can be a very fruitful, necessary experience or solution for a number of Black Americans. I am more interested in what you might call the cultural move, the spiritual move, even the intellectual move."

And, in some ways, that is what this is about really: culture. This is more than a collection of poems to me; these are building blocks saying, we write what we like and we made this for you. I like Okot p'Bitek and ain't notin wrong wit dat.

From this line, this line, this line here, here, we rebuild. Rebuild, rebuild Afrika. I write what I like.

Steve Biko: "You are either alive and proud or you are dead, and when you are dead, you can't care anyway."

I Write What I Like.

"Being black is not a matter of pigmentation—being black is a reflection of a mental attitude."

I Write What I Like.

"Merely by describing yourself as black you have started on a road towards emancipation, you have committed yourself to fight against all forces that seek to use your blackness as a stamp that marks you out as a subservient being."

I Write What I Like.

"The most potent weapon in the hands of the oppressor is the mind of the oppressed."

I write what I like and I made this, for you.

JAMBALAYA

Jambalaya
Salif Keita in the morning sun

Tswana eyes,
My bare feet in the airport.

--

It is a pain in my gut
I need to see you,
I fiend like a junkie in a tub
A secretary bird kicking the skulls and snakes

Pillowcases and sheets
Dangling out of government windows
To be with you in the moon's court,
Jurors of stars, vindicating my love

Rock paintings on cracked skin
I leap with kudus
Clear cross the Atlantic
Like arrows of the San

--

Guava eyes
Running kickball in a dirt arena,
Ribbons of trash waving like cheering crowds

Donkeys abused by schoolchildren
Donkeys dead in the dust

In the city, the cattle belong to the people.
In the village and at the cattle post,
They belong to the people.

In Africa the sky is higher.

At night
I dragged three kitchen chairs between screen doors
And placed them in the yard to lie underneath the stars

Under the stars;

Floodlights on divinity

--

Chobe, Sedudu: a lagoon at night,
An obsidian screen of stars with islands of water plants

Rolled trouser cuffs, rowing a raft
Origami in the delta
Between hippos that stud the water like mines

--

And now I sit in the desert
Trying to remember my stories,
A million zebras rushing through my head

--

I hunger in the light—a baby turtle on the sand
The deafening cry of seagulls above,
Flippers puffing the sand,
The sea,
Maybe another four hundred years away

Dear Afrika,
It took me four hundred years to understand
That I love you,
And I miss you very much

TUCK SHOP CIPHER

I.

Tuck Shop cipher
American litter between our toes
As we tread through plastic water

Pumping Heinz over seswaa and pap
Gazing over the tumours of Gaborone
We scratch and pick

Downtown,
Women bleach the melanin off their skin:
Black goddesses ...

to filleted fish

We hunt shopping malls
Oiling our fingers with New York Fries
And come out,

ON-AIR!

Americans broadcasting "Children of the Slum"

In American-made slums

2 A.M.,

By the shebeen,

Kwaito vibrating the marble sky

Yellow grocery bags swirling outside a foreign-owned shop

tilted hat, Thabo Pacino

10 thebe rolling across the knuckles, director's cut

Jolts of gunfire

Batswana explode out of the bar

Mardi Gras of broken glass

a body.

2.

Barclays Bank in the town square, next to Just Bread

Deep baskets of mopane, sculpture carving on the street

I swivel in the barber's chair as he points to hip-hop posters,

"Sharp"

The empresses smile shyly as I walk out—

Rubbing alcohol still on my forehead.

Holding a meat pie, watching South African soap operas
The hotel shower curtain new and glistening,
We make our way downstairs
To passion fruit juice under an open roof,
Safari dinner, steel kegs under Amazon palms.

Tomorrow we'll look for a house and school ...

Tall grasses, hissing insects
My baggy jeans tripping over a ground tap
As uniforms assemble in the dust

The first day, I was introduced,
On steel chairs at the back of the classroom

"Yannick, meet your intellectual equal and poet-friend,
Your 'back-of-the-classroom jokers,'
And your first kiss"

And the prodigal son,
The Pan-Africanist paramour,

found a reason to write poetry again.

WHERE JAZZ MEETS THE CITYSCAPE

Peppercorn head, I remember you,
With eyes so bright, like dilated asterisks
Pleading at car doors by Woolworths

--

Here, Jazz meets the Cityscape
And obelisks of heritage I've brought back to y'all
Kente cloths of afro-centrism
"Here! Look! I've found myself"

--

H.I.V. punctures a people
Like raindrops on cobwebs,
They wake up early
And tie latex banners in the street to stop the flood

That wasn't my concern;

It was the first time I heard "Laku Tshoni 'Ilanga"
I was leaning on the tuck shop with loving eyes
When she clicked her tongue and took her stock sweets,
And I followed that walk,

To bricks that served as benches
Where she let me put desert flowers in her hair

(The slums, the hospice—
blurred in dilated pupils)

--

Now wherever I go
The buildings smoke

Big red buildings, the Gangsta Industrialists;
The moonlight is a syringe to the concrete
Where we freestyle on trashcans
Neo-soul hats and brick walls
Where Jazz meets the Cityscape

And all I want to do—

Is adorn you

SHALL WE?

Shall we?
Hustle into horse and carriage
And leave London for the brown-capped boys
Walking through white spiders of rain,
Are you ready to shut out the slums,
the mills, the factories?
And let the scenery mist against your face
As England rolls its credits?
Cuz, when the plane lands
And we walk down the stairs
We'll be like children reunited with fathers,
Children who've been gone too long,
And we won't need brochures,
No brochures, we're home,
Afrika will loosen your collar and take off your shoes,
It will be a cold shower after a long day's work,
There will be trees with better shade,
Shade that knows how to shade us,
Hasn't it been too long?
Cheers to London, salut to France,
But, black people, it's been too long

SINAI

Cogs of snowflakes,
Icing ground, Goliath trudging behind,
Sleighs slicing, ground writhing below,
We *iz*

Lips quaking, sucking raw seal,
Kinks silvering in the sleet
JAH!

Solidify these bones, these heels
Bare on tundra

Remember these backs
With scars swollen to serpents

Remember these fathers
Letting first-borns slip into the sea
Like parachutes, sinking
Bouncing on the heads of humpbacks

Remember this people
Like water pouring back into Your hands

We stiffen to sleet
And clatter

Clatter

NOMAD

Where do I rest?
When my head is crowded and all light seems dim,
The bread is stale; the water is dried up,
Sand dunes deep, trails of camels few amidst
The endless desert ...
I long for hints of orange rinds
Pineapple punch, and shade,
Give me vines for chains,
Grapes, feed my camels,
Treacherous sun, devouring all hope,
Can there be deliverance?
Or eternal suffering,
Who has made my skin into parched clay?

No, no, no, the sun beats more
Has lynched me a thousand times and left me to dry,
No, no, I lust for water
Scaled fingers lining a goat-skinned rim,
Is this the only delusion that can be afforded me?
Sun and sand,
The terrors of continuous distance, sand and sand again?
What lives and does not dry?
What breathes breath finer than smoke?
Is there no deliverance?

I'm like a captured cow, feet tied to a pole,
Thinking of greener days, tambourines, and musicians
At the mercy of the young girls,
I'm like a cow, seeing for the first time the world upside-down
The sky a low and brooding desert,
Where is the clap of hands? The missing teeth?
The animals? Is this the end?
If I fall face first into the sand
Will there be nothing changed?
No hair on the neck of eternity stir?
The night is cooler than its touch;
The days chase me in chariots,
Laugh after me, Oh treacherous, treacherous sun.

I have travelled far with a hunched back,
Pitied by winds, scorned by rain,
Limping from where I came to where I wish to go,
A black man whose nature attracts sun,
I have left those who robbed me
But by my scars, I lose hope
That my own will know me

Hear me now, pain, take all my tears from me,
No thunder, no, no crash of clouds,
The hunger that pulls on the gut of the world
Has me trapped in the centre,

I shall chisel the tears from my cheek
Before I let you into my bed
With your love's tales

Bow heavy head, fear no more the heat of the sun,
Hands drag like some Neanderthal-like sorrow,
There's an end to all thirst
A river at the end of all journeys,
Forget the tambourines that beat orange,
Release your chest from your clench
And mock all joy, scoff at all weakness,
Lay your head down on this rock,
And rest awhile.

TO THE CONTINENTAL AFRIKAN

Push your hand,
through my hair.

Search savannahs at midnight, orchards of black broccoli.
Afro mane, black smoke and static crowning
marbled skin. White blood perforating ebony,
Milk, curdling black limestone, but

Ancestors purify with each pulse,
Chlorine-cleansing
the defilement of yokels.

Hear thin rains over nappy-headed mountains,
Green shrubs concealing Maroon villages. Glass pregnancies
in fingernails bearing grounded dirt, cane sugar
tickling diastema. White crab
crushed in bathwater as swelling infants rise
under drained coconuts,
umbilical cords buried beneath silk cotton trees.

Lips thick as roast breadfruit, kissing fetishes
and stowaway gods shrivelled by slavers' moons.
Twilight incantations drawing geese
from kidney-coloured etherlands.

Goatskin stretched to drum, resounding in velvet skies.
White robes, pious, for night-baptism
in okra wine.

Eyes of halved limes: green buggy wheels
serrating trough water. North star of a teal night
replacing bone marrow with longing
as welts deep like pockets furrow skin.
Pupils flashing histories
of whips,
of home

Push your hand
through my hair,
brother.

I am who I am

NEO-SOUL

neo-soul, afro queen

we vegetarian,
bok choy, steamed grass in shallow water

you bring beauty out
like champagne from a bucket of ice

i toast to the alchemy of your skin
crushed and drawn with milk,

you touch me like gospel

THE SUN IS GOING DOWN

The sun is going down,
Making snakeskin of taps running cold water
Over your temples as you wash your locks,

I come with a bag of seashells and
Put them in the sink,
You smell of kerosene and papaya,
Black Dutch pots whistling on the fire ...

My mind jumps broomsticks
To take yours to bed,
When the rain makes your signal weak,

And invites you to a mattress
Under a roof massacred
By shotgun shells of stars,

Then,

I'd watch your words tilt like fedoras
And trace the aurora borealis
Through the lattice of your eyes
Seeing sugar cane fields, coconuts and rye ...

And I'd cautiously step,
Through the wheat fields as you slept,
Bringing the moon in a wheelbarrow,

Leaving tracks in your subconscious
And sprawling out beneath the groves
With a straw hat and twig between my teeth
Sailing my hand across a dimming world,

As you awake

To the beams of running water

NDOKO

Blackness is more than beauty;
It is wings on water,
Two Ba birds,
In flight to Kemet

Twin shoulders, black Kilimanjaros,
To the valley and slope of her neck

Her skin is health to my fingers,
Diasporic marble, sands of disrupted kingdoms
Melted to dark sugar,
Organic, untainted

Full lips
Whose touch blows through my body
As if I were made of bedsheets

Wisps of dry grass tangled in our hair
From sleeping in the savannah,
Our soft drumming,
Raising butterflies from tall grass

We turn over,

Our indigo spilt from the night sky,
Tar-love in the fields

I tear the tendons of this language
And pile them on her altar,
The smoke
Simmering the red sun ...

Our Blackness is more than beauty,
It is two Ba birds circling the horizon
Parallel

Until the dip
                          The dive
                                         The vanishing

Into blackness

TROPIC

Jamaica rained
black umbrellas necked
as couples found shelter in the shadows,
the moon, shining
with the mist of stars sprayed around her
like a freshly diced lime,

and you were poetryed,
with almonds that I was to consider eyes,
with ginger that I was to consider skin,
spicing that intoxicating swirl of night.

stars. sea. palm trees.
the rise and fall of sandy beaches embodied in your curves.
i'd wade knee-deep in coconut water
to the place of open sea
where poets tug their anchors out from depths
to drift over your waters.

yes,
the moon,
it is shining,
dusting the sky like squeezed lime, spraying
over the love-act,

till we sleep

waiting
        for the cry

of gulls.

A POEM INSPIRED BY AFRIKAN SCENERY

My sickle's limp with the weight of love;
My hands seek your palm wine—
They're dry like stale milk and barley,
You are the love child; I am the fits of passion,
The mules can't drag the weight of love
Love stales milk; it dries barley,
It is the ale of good times,
It is the liquor of worse.
My sickle's limp with the weight of love,
Bent, in the reaper's wheat fields.

SEA CRABS

Sea crabs, on white sands reflecting,
Some wood's burning, hear the crackles?

Sitting under the thatched roof, the waterfall
Of stars on the beach, and callaloo
Steamed for you and I to dine tonight
With coconut wine and whispers ...

Or we can sip green leaf tea
And hold hands along the coast,
Watching reeds calling for fishermen,
And the sea moaning for unseen gulls,

We'll laugh like lovers

Until the water-stars are gathered and lost—
On the shores of St. Lucia

INSHALLAH

Dravidians mouthing Sanskrit limericks
On rose-decked oak wood tables,
Night-blue beaches, translucent crabs
Drowning
In whisky-suppers

I am marooned,
Viewing her lesser constellations,
From the Lesser Antilles

Her love was guava,
Lime trees glistened under crescent eyes
Leaves brushing half-moons,
Caramel skin, scented with rum punch
And a kindness
That drew pigeons to feet

Love is a very hard thing to kill

So,
I'll make my love a circle,
And wait till you come round again

EDEN

There is a blue-green tide filled with urchins, seahorses, and tropical fish that washes over the island's sand like magic. We used to come down to this beach, Kizzy, Chelsea, Eden, and I, to bathe and play. Tourists always talk about the beaches. They never talk about picking up a Kellogg's Corn Flakes from the centre aisle in M. Baptiste's supermarket. Or how the salt has been spilt on a steel shelf, circling the old flour bags who sit as dreary as pets in a pet store.

"Do you have any salt beef?" M. Baptiste came out from behind the counter and drew the last of the salt beef from the bloody white bucket. He wrapped it in a brown sheet of paper and handed it to me.

"Tell your mother I will pray for her," he said, returning to his work. I thanked him enthusiastically and assured him we would pay him back.

I ran from the supermarket all the way down High Street. Flowers were blown all over Castries like the end of carnival; the wind mashed up many of the rooftop antennas. I had the mint leaves and the salt beef and still had change to bring back to my mother. Chickens squawked above white '85 Toyota car-roofs, sweating men drew machetes and held green coconuts to the sun while I counted the change.

The glass doors of the clinic-pharmacy were always shining, blurred forms flapped newspapers, or tapped prescription bottles inside. I open the doors to find Madame Meda speaking with a stranger.

"Oh my Doodoo, come and sit, how is your mother?" Madame Meda was always over my head like a fat hummingbird.

I acknowledged her friend with a nod and replied, "She is doing fine, Madame, she has enough strength to walk now." Madame said something about her keeping my mother in her prayers, but my mind was already distracted, scanning the aisle for Tylenol.

I thanked Madame, kissed her on her cheek and picked up the medicine. An old man opened the glass doors of the pharmacy. I caught a glimpse of my cousin between the old man's cane and his weak hip; my cousin was kicking a ball down the other side of the street.

"Eden!" I shouted.

I ran through the street, Dr. Chin screaming after me, and heaven growling with indigestion above me.

"Eden! You know how sick my mother is? Where have you been? Come back home right now!" He continued to kick the ball.

"EDEN!" I screamed into his ear, but it was hollow like the beaches.

I jumped onto the back of a van and bumped all the way to Balata's hill. At home, Auntielera was stirring a pot of boillion on the stove, lizards camouflaged near the flakes in the wallpaper. I gave her the mints and the salt beef and walked past the kitchen calendar to my mother's bedroom. My mother was sleeping with a hot water bottle on her chest and a spinning fan by her bedside. I placed two capsules in her water and watched them sizzle. I nudged my mother awake.

"Mother, I saw Eden playing—running out of the city today."

She smiled and drank the water.

PROCESSION TO DILAPIDATIONS

Scarecrow magic, late in the field,
When dark men jump picket fences, leaving trails of country
    bourbon
As the red barn heaves its breath into the night

Rain falls like miracles on the road,
Polishing cornstalks with moonlight;
Down the gutter of roofs like squeezed lime,
Wild rain is the dreadlocks of heaven

Extinguished lighter smoke chalks the night,
We feel the beat squishing between our toes while
Women drape over our shoulders like listless sunshine

Coming in from the party:
Flip-flops, swaggers, and drawls,
Hiccups freckle the air like ripped cardboard
As delayed jokes resume their tickle

Flies bunx the kitchen lights

Out the door, four feet search for the grass
Crescent on the veranda: love's haiku

The moon printed on the dark sky like a stuffed beetle,
Scythes already killing the canes,
Carried on straw hats, through the sweet water

The canes fall like shot men—
Through the sweet, green, Caribbean water

KINGSTON LIGHT

The fishmongers come on Tuesday,
Smelling like papaya seeds and saltfish
While schoolboys play football, trying to impress
The young girls with neatly plaited hair, who would settle
To walk home rather than press through minibus passengers.

The surrounding markets have stands as brittle
As sugar cane, yet support the strong black elbows
Of quarrelling Ms. O'Neil, who is sure she gave
Twenty dollars change to an unconvinced Ms. Reynolds.

This is Kingston Light
Somebody heard shots but no, this is Kingston Light

The Rastaman and his staff,
Trodding to the riddim of some ancient bongo drums,
A car passes—Mr. Channer kisses his teeth:
"Why dem bwoy nah go dung a August Town an' play dem ting?
Dem nah see nobody wan 'ear dat boogo boogo music round yah"
Rice and peas and oxtail are served in a thatched restaurant
Moist under plastic wrap. The pineapple sun streams nectar on
        veranda plants
Drawing hummingbirds to ackee-flowered tables, till they fly out
        over the street

Where goat herders lead their goats through rivers of cars and
    soldier jeeps.

Street dogs, rummaging through discarded okra skins
Looking for traces of Bully Beef. "Red Stripe" billboards
Picket against a descending sun. Blue mountains guard
Sandcastles by the sea; under the umbrella of seawater mists
That carry moths in orbit to houses on the hill

This is Kingston Light
Somebody heard shots but no, this is Kingston Light

When fried fish is bagged by diligent black fingers,
When the peanut punch trickles down the satisfied grins of children,
When the preachers shout over plastic barrels on dusty roads,
When dominoes slam tables in the sun hot—
Till the rain comes, which drives the schoolers home
And half drowns the distant sounds of reggae music.

When the sun come up bright, bright, bright

Somebody heard shots but no,

This is Kingston Light
Kingston Light
Kingston Light.

SOMETIMES I FEEL LIKE MY HEAD IS GATHERING WATER

Sometimes I feel like my head is gathering water,
And sailboats,
With the dome of stars like sweat on a black-skinned night
Rippling under the surf

The moon drawing me just like magnet to steel
Over sand dissected by tire tracks
Where I trod softly,
So as not to crush the tin backs of tender-fleshed crabs
Returning to salt water
Like diced potatoes slipping into soup

Sometimes I feel like
My head is gathering water,
Gathering like a fisherman casting his seine into the sea,
Not for the fish, but for the blue sky–filled droplets left on the mesh

And when my head is swooshing,
Between my ears, swirling

And my eyes well up with paradise
Rusting to corrugated iron

Sometimes I feel as though

Me head
      A gadda

              Wata

And I'm set adrift
Under the dome of stars
In my home   away from home   away from home

MOUNTAIN KINGDOM PASTORAL

1. Mountain kingdom pastoral

ascending a donkey trail,
the Mountain View opens the mouth of our eyes—

we suckle like children seizing at God's salt and peppered beard,
aging masterfully with snow, jutting hillside tree, shrub,
our mouths grow big like our eyes.

we've climbed, the stars beneath us,
we gaze down into the quiet-time of the countryside.

Right there,
Mohale water as clear as this land is beautiful,
feeds a dam suckling twins

Mountain kingdom Harmattan sweeps its dirt, snow about
    blanketed bodies,
Mohale's Hoek whistles as an open-air flute.

Over there,
herders steeped in blankets ferry flocks
in from the wind to the valleys,
one boy, drinking another herder's donkey milk,

hearing his nearing scream disappears into Lesotho night,
under cover of wind and dark
as villages pack back into their bellies,
like meat made with three-legged pots.

the mountains, the hills—they all have names, you know

From here,
Lesotho stretches like African sky,
blanketed by a mountain range of dignified elders,
posing as an inverted flotilla of cloud
under a starlit sea of sky

2. *Of drought and chieftains*

and that night we awoke,
seeking water for bucket like a man proposing
marriage
to the father, for the daughter's hand.

we'd, whilst trudging, realized nothing, reconciled
nothing,
and as such, we broke our bucket.
animals scavenged about the veld yelling,
"moisture!! moisture!! ... the grass is brown"

and so there we were, bucket broke,
parched, bickering upon chapping broken lips,
and i'm ashamed to say,
my chieftaincy was in doubt—

for we were to have waited till six,
or the decommissioning of rations, before walking,

for with Ramadan in the moon
"God surely would be with us"
walking in search of water,

it rained
and it was as if the sky were kissing an inverted
mountain—
sky kissing mountain kingdom

and so there we were,
I, in my second year digging pit latrines,
some in their fourth straight year in drought,

only the children played in the rain,
their frames wrestling with inventoried droplets

some of us, somewhat older, knew
the rain, irreverent as to our need,

would visit Mohale like a woman with marriage
arranged,
only to elope with another

the tiny droplets each catalogued,
their little labels read,
"Property of the Republic of South Africa"

HURRICANE

Sleep, sweetly.

On orange peels
In the aroma of boiled basmati.

Pray, sweetly.

That if we take flight,
Our house will find its route
Among the fairies.

STORMVIEW

the world splits into fragmented rain
life becomes jagged
projectile homes,
torsos of trees

our bodies cling, rural
countrysides in deep embrace
as the sky dries its head over the basin of stars,
our bodies move,
you and i,
decomposing into torrents, lightning
weaving its bright webs around us
as we slush, sludge to the mountainside

and then
it ends

and starfish return to water-dancing
mocking their celestial counterparts;
manicous unfurl and warm their bellies on the rocks
and you and i,
our bodies like countrysides loosened from each other
return to separate hills
distant hills

look up,
a puzzle blown to pieces—

fragments of God

GRENADA GIRL

over dem hills dey,
her night-village does shine,
like a grave of peenie-wallie

and at nights we would sleep together
blanketed by the scent of nutmeg
and the calls of warner women on the hills

and so we, and many others, slept,
in colourful shacks all over the spice island,
inhaling the cloves of night's aroma,
perfumed with peace

and after watching us sleep so, so sweet so,
in our sweet-scented villages,
Night became jealous,
and say to himself say,

"You know? Me nuh like Grenada yuh know,
Me nuh like her at all, at all"

and rub his black black hands and start wuk him obeah
all ova mi gal

and that night it was still, still till morning
still, cause Wind was picking the grime from him toenails
and dashing it way out a sea,
him yawn, scratch him balls,
and say to Night say, "A wha dat yuh tell me fi go do again?"
Night point to Grenada,
hear Wind

"yes, yes,"

and Wind push out one long, tuff, foot down to the shore and
        whisper,

"Me deh yah"

and clouds start swirl like when poco women ketch spirit,
fishmongers were pelted with starfish, anemones covered their
        children's ears
and tumbled softly through the streets,
parrots dove under lime trees, green wings over green heads
as Yemoja played Mas, ponging zinc roofs like steel pans,
and the whole island was jumping up, jumping up,
red, green, and gold curtains waving like flags
as the spice isle was plunged and drawn, plunged and drawn
from involuntary steambaths, puffing us into sky ...

and I clinged to her toe
while she somersaulted between the stars,
limbo stance,
praying to the moon

and I thought she was dead.

but there she was,

in her Grenada dress,
with her soul of the Caribbean,

(an a soh yuh do me darlin,
all when yuh a *mash* me up, mi deh yah still, don't it?

a jus soh yuh do me darlin
yuh soul sweet so till)

IROKO

Who carpeted Mama's womb with bush fire,
That she would shed her skin and tears just for me?

As I evolved within her closed circuit,
Scraping the spark-branches from her nape to navel.

Who smoked me out?
Brought panic to my fetus till it shuddered between her?

Iroko.

Beautiful bark,
shelter and nourishment.

Raw trail of yolk that sanctified this germ,
That brought man out of matter.

Iroko.

That diced the night within her belly walls
Spoon-feeding me dreams of the constellations.

Gave me an abacus of her joints
To calculate each spasm, draw each gasp.

She groaned,
As I reared my head lizard-like
Scanning this new orphanage.

What welcome is this?
Into white hands initiating me into this vileness
When I used to string the planets like beads around my head?

Who has summoned me from the lamp,
And has given this anthology of thought form?

Iroko,
don't let them take me!
Expand your belly skin and let me grow as a man within you,

Iroko,
uproot,

take me back to the sun.

TWO NAPPY HEADS

Two nappy heads running at my waist,
My boys, with pieces of coconut in their mouths ...
I want them to grow tall, so tall
They'd have to bend under the telephone wires,
I want them to stretch through my fingers
And draw their communities from deep water

I want my baby to be like her mother, secure,
Never second guessing her intelligence nor her beauty,
I want men to hold her in a respectful fear
As she educates the streets
With the grace of her walk,
I want her to have questions and need no answers,
Even as she does, here,
Curdling in my arms like milk

I want my community
To get from under the hair dryer
And bust it to pieces!
Breathing in the true, Afrikan cosmology,
And know that it has nothing to do with being kings or queens,
But that our *self* —
Is our affirmation

And I want my Afrikans to love themselves
With a passion so strong it makes them sleepy,
Enough to stumble and yawn
Through the whips of any oppressor

And I'd love to wait and watch for it,
But my home is the Dogon cliffs
With the griots, and the preservers of truth,
Where as far as my eyes can see, the world's
Whimpering with love

A SERVICE AT GRANT AFRICAN METHODIST EPISCOPAL CHURCH

Preach Pastor, Preeeeach On, Brother!! Sunday bests, suits and boots stomping church-pews cuz the spirit is live, bustin epiphanies down aisles hands clenching bonnets fo the holy ghost run loose, let loose, get loose up in here. Alright cool, take your seats and cool, like some water, cool. The spirit is live, on fire; church brochures turn to fans in the dead of winter. Scotians packed to the ceiling, molasses heaving heavy chested over the pews.

My mind drifts to jazz or blues, or that crawfish, or that crayfish swooshing in paper bags as Negroes tugged Negroes through that underground. That underground lit by crosses, and freedom, and spirituals, and spirits, whisky and song drugging the passage. Offering plates passing secret messages tucked into bosoms, blossoming in cedar coffins slippin through Quaker carriages. My mind drifts to jazz, scat scatting with the preacher, pastor, preacher's raspy voice when we make music, he tappin the altar, me tappin the ground, he tappin the mic, he tappin the soul, me scatting with a velvet hat, velvet suit, coulda had a velvet-tipped shoe, we drift to jazz.

Blues, ain't it something how a people can go through something like all that, and still squeeze bibles like sponges, like sponges or rags dabbed across foreheads? Beading sweat, hot, worked sweat, women bending back, arms wide open, awaiting God, awaiting salvation, sweet smelling, jackfruit, baked bread, blackberry pie salvation drifting low, swinging low from heaven's window sill.

Nah, low, take it low, you know like how she sang, how she sang it out, sang His eye was on the sparrow, sang "oh yes," sang "don't tell God how big your storm is, tell your storm how big your God is" sang. OH what a friend we have in Jesus, who keeps our wrists wringing and our bellies busting with that deep country town fried chicken apple cider grab a hold a somethin fo you fall music, OH what a friend. Nah take it low, take it low like the altar call where hands rise and cry "Oh yes Lawd," "OH thank you JESUS!!" And the organ pipes sigh, and the ushers comfort, and the tears gather, streak and fall into handkerchiefs. Nah, take it low, make it hum to ya, hum to ya, hum.

It's you that kept us, your cedar walls, your fiery sermons, it's you that kept us, gathered our tears, bent your back when we made like falling. Your choirs, your gospels, your hot, steel, Bible. Preserver. We salute you.

AFRICVILLE: THE RELOCATION

It was a gaseous belch from whisky-stained God
That brought Nova Scotia's slum into existence.
We held our breath that night—
when the stars smelled like sardines
an the moon was a puddle of vodka.

That night we held our noses and flung
Bottles and curses into the air
Because God didn't say excuse me.
God was just listening to his radio
When we suffered in his stench,
Staining the slums of Africville.

That's why the Canucks came. For sanitary
Reasons they said, it was a stain, God's belch,
On all of Nova Scotia. So they came in with mops
To wash us away. We said, covering our noses, that
We could stand the stench, we said, climbing pails and
Mop hair, we will stand the stench. But they polished us,
Shined us into paved places, hymnless congregations
Shuffling under God's fish-greened breath. They polished us,
They soap-and-watered us out of our homes.

And just to think, we, under the beam of midnight trains

Stealing underground, we, were corpses in birch boxes
Chugging under stenches to canada's freedom. We corpsed,
Under the terrible stench of God's gaseous emissions for days and
    days,
Nova Scotia's belch of night leading us like shadows over water.
For many, many nights we held our noses, we could stand the stench,
And now I cannot find my baby in the crowd. Relocated
In the gaseous stench of projects, Halifax garbage, holding
Our noses looking for our babies in the crowd.

CECILIA

Hear now, take what you will of raspberries,
Take the light of the moon; it's late—
The gondolas need sleep, and Italy
Has no need of stirring. Let us part, now,
Let us not wake the clocks—force tolls and chimes
Against us. Night washes over Venice,
Taking ports, and docks, and city lights.
You, whored by lanterns, bob and sway,
Bob and look far out to sea

The salt breeze knows it,
The shutting casements high above us know it,
The coastguards on their watch, know—
It's late.

ALIENATION

In the streets we astro-project,
Lifted by lead,
Pressed against the troposphere
Like insects under glass roofs,

they float out
To ghettoize the heavens

The universe is a project sink, infested,
Steel roaches propelled into a cosmic drain—
Stardust flaking
Like lice in an Afro

Planets burst,
Red explosions in celestial bodies—
Waiting for comets to circle the block like sirens

The moon sick on the curb,
Sniffing rocks,
Shivering,
Vomiting Milky Ways

Down here they walk among us
Surveillance on every street corner,
Examining our behaviour in city-wide incubators,
Observing our resilience to painful stimuli

People get shot out of windows
Raptured into the sky like disco balls

Nothing's new,
The streets is *The Matrix*

ALL THE TIME IN THE GHETTO, VIOLENCE

you can't spin on the taps
there's a drought in the city;
blacks swarm the city's junk spots like flies

there is a phenomenal aura
beneath the subway-in-the-sky,
your jacket holds tighter to you
as you play
red light, green light,
with shivering addicts

at the ball cage
young men feel out the firmness of black thighs
as girls feign resistance
to commodification

the run:
bare chests pulsing with sound systems,
shouts, scrape of sneakers on a tar court,
till a wavelength moves through the block
and the crowd parts like hair

watch,
you can trace the bullet with a pencil

to the point of impact,
the gnashing teeth,
the head butting the ground,
the bulging eyes
and the blood flattening the cement like
an emasculated balloon

then the evening turns pink—

and mothers sit by the body
like ampersands

SONNET FOR MY CRACK PRINCESS

Red vegetables are on her plate,
She watches moons that shine like Chrysler chrome
Through swinging gates, and sparse tufts of grass,
Holding her baby like a bushel of wheat,
Over cocaine skin, sifting the rain.
Dad's gone like swinging gates.

I skip across the water with a bucket of ice
And look into her eyes of Las Vegas;
To where I'd dangle from her thoughts like an IV,
Kissing the naps back down her forehead,
Digging gardens in the small of her back
Until she ... black out like electricity

Get out of here let me get her a basin,
You will not see us here again.

BAGGA BALLAD

For you ...

I would crush mosquitoes before their moonlanding
And let them pastel into the sunset.

I would take the glass from your heel
And replace all of the stars.

I would tie a hammock between government buildings
And make us an embassy of rain.

And when it pours sea-urchin spines
Leaving mirrors in cement,

I will uproot this ghetto;
For you, I'll tilt the sea.

LIBERATION

Songs burst in my head,
I'd like to slip these words over the pew,
To you,
A love-bridge over maniacal preaching

Whenever there are sirens
Staining the glass,
Red, white, and blue butterflies
Fluttering over a body

Whenever there are notices
And couches out in the yard,
And this sanctuary is a shelter,
From the nitrogen blasts of winter moons

Whenever there are mouths to feed,
Fingertips glistening with saliva,
Cleaned saucers swirling on a table
Under eyes that understand

I will breathe old Negro spirituals down your neck,
Grinding rough skin to coffee,
Loosening the lace from your turquoise hat,
And the pins from your tight-bunned hair

And you will whisper,
"Yes preacher yes, yes preacher ..." Amen,
Let it be a smooth, smooth road
Down to Jordan

TO MY BABYMOTHER

Mmm. So I woulda never leave if it wasn't winter. If the snow never
marched over the sidewalks, and if your mittened hands never
pushed shopping carts through the slush. I woulda did deh. Mmm.
And true night-snow will not stop fall like white babies onto black
nannies. And true the wind will not stop splash ice water beneath
your parka. I tell you I woulda did deh. If even for her, wrapped
in your arms like a snowcone. If even for the leaks dripping into
the puddle by your bedside, where slipper-prints trail to a door of
blizzards.

I neva gwaan bout no love ting. There were two heads, two feet,
two wings as we made snow angels on patterned sheets. Now it's
funny how we can make a life, shape a life then let it melt like ice
sculptures in your womb. And how you neva so much as sigh as
snow cascaded into your pupils. Nuttin I can give, nuttin more than
day-old snow and tufts of dead grass I can give you. Nuttin when
your bare foot is chained to icicles and the cruisers are out of reach.
Nuttin when the world is nuttin but hoots from white snow and
snow owls and snow owls. You neva gwaan bout no love ting but you
were with me still, making what was frozen and dead into a river.

Now if I held her hand, closed it in mine like a tiny maple leaf,
we would both break apart. Her, because her tree was never well
rooted, and me, because I am made of wind. If she could feel out the

form of my features, and know intimately every inadequacy then she wouldn't have no dream. I would be a cellar door slamming between her frosted stars. I would be pried apart like birch bark and she would see the empty, sapless flesh. No, I will be the one that will customize her moons, remove my face and let the stars be her mobile.

I want these words to touch your fingers. I want them to be warm like the hum of refrigerators. I want them to find pity, though they will parch your throat and be pins into your heart. I want them to console like dial tones after a while, true—after a long, angry, while. I cannot rationalize what is only guilt and fear. I cannot smother the hisses of all who read this. But of all the tears that flow, I want some that are partial to me, want one that streams down warm, for me.

So I'm counting my tokens, and I have my bags. And true the snow's lighter now, pirouetting off the noses of sewer pipes. True the sky is a laundry grey and the suds are collecting on toques and window frames. But it's still winter. And mi still—*trodding tru dis country to rahtid*. Me did deh still. And the snow *will* fall, cascading from your pupils, but the winds will die. And she will grow, perhaps slightly hollow but made with tougher bark. True I'm gone, but *everything is everything*. Blessed. I'm sorry to leave your door to this blizzard.

WAITING FOR METRO

i)

i have a gun
in a Hardo Bread bag

waiting for Metro marching from the marshlands of Suburbia,
to occupy our lands

waiting

the snails will no longer be crushed,
by black boots

ii)

my sister was sleeping in my mother's car at the GO station,
you came pounding at the window:

"what are you doing here?"

"there have been thefts"

"where does your mother work?"

"why don't you walk home"

it was 1 in the morning,
we live past a dark park,
over quiet streets,
where nobody's daughter should walk

iii)

i carry a gun
in a Hardo Bread bag

for the ones and ones who are accidentally murdered by police,
who are handcuffed, billy-clubbed, prostrated on gravel,
for the ones who are bled and hung from apartment balconies,
where mothers with rollers in their hair
leave pots of curry, bend under telephone wire clotheslines
and bawl,
look out through the traffic smog and bawl

i carry a gun
for those whose blood police carry back to the mayor in buckets,
to wash down the TTC,
to scrub the pigeon shit from the streets,
to baptize white liberalism

iv)

i have a gun
in a Hardo Bread bag

to protect against white women
who lament that Toronto is becoming Jane and Finch,
Albion Mall, Regent Park

who squeeze their purse
when we walk past them to the back of the bus

v)

we run from police—

above Ojibwa faces cemented in the sidewalks
their totems crouching beneath the power lines

we jump walls, we lay in alleys, we slip
under cover of city smog,
until the sun comes up and we slink out into the streets,
like shell-less snails shivering under the shadow
of black boots

vi)

one day you will look out your window
and we will be there, the loyalist slaves,
knee-length rags, tufts of prairie grass in our hair
standing in your cool, cool Suburbia

we will be there, noose in hand,
hiding behind your blue-bins,

heart beating with the tantrum of a terrorist

vii)

i have a gun
in a Hardo Bread bag

Mau Mau dreads
soaked with the Talmud
sprinkled atop my head from Kemetic pitchers

happy shall he be, that taketh and dasheth thy little ones against
    the stones,
headlong into their lemonade stands,
pushing them off their tricycles,
yes,

happy shall he be, that taketh and dasheth thy little ones against
    the stones

viii)

and if I am a racist,
I am a realist

ix)

i have a gun
in a Hardo Bread bag

Because as sure as autumn makes sunsets of the maple's leaves,
As sure as the loon's call will forever haunt the great canadian lakes,
As sure as the white wolf sings to the great white moon

we will kill you

PEEPHOLE

It's ten past ten and she's washing dresses,
Waiting for him to come home,
To glimpse till next August gumboots,

To hear her mine bird knocking on those old plastic bag windows
    like he used to

She's waiting to tell Joe to call Go-go,
To say, there's much to celebrate, Ghibo

She's waiting to see him walking across the street
Juxtapose to where the power goes
Giving small sweets to Joe for running so fast, Calling Go-go

She's looking out into the night
Into its big, beautiful, dark blue eyes
She wonders

Watching Joe cut through Mrs. Modise's chicken-wire fencing
Like it's a school day,
Afraid to ask him what exactly he thinks he's doing,
Twisting it back like a braid,
Running toward the shebeen in those big, beautiful, dark blue eyes,
Mrs. Modise screaming—

Voices calling out

She's watching Joe *"Shake-Shake!"* back, forth,
Chibuku thick on his jaw,
Untwisting the braid,
Re-twisting it like school's out,

She's looking out at the proximity of the township,
Breathing into someone's face—
She hears the scandal—
On whose house has the home scooped out like pulp
On whom not to visit until the preacher says the community should
        rally

She looks out into the night—
Into its big, beautiful, dark blue eyes
She's washing his shirt, waiting for him to come home,
Hug her like he used to,
Coughing, losing weight, her tuberculosis as bad as ever
Waiting for ten o'clock,
For the non-generic feel,
That ol' take me while you have me,
Anti-retroviral
Lamivudine

THE ART OF POISON

They're killing us slowly,
Shrieks on a wet road, shacks watching like prisoners
As AIDS beats another family to powder

From city lights to the farmlands
Napalm travels to our blood,
Through traffic lights, on wagons,
Leeches are dumped in the drinking water
Till we're sucked dry
And ribs prod through skin
Like wildebeest carcasses

Flamingos perched on the traffic lights
Bending their wings to make the moonlight rose-coloured
As children are ushered to cardboard boxes on the streets of Harare,
Gassed stomachs and pink foot-bottoms,
Mauve geckos scattered over the markets like old vegetables

By the shed's light,
(Making toilet bowl water an impressionist painting),
She waits like a model in a window,
For a man that will make her body forget the heat,
They crash onto a springless mattress,
Pumping each other like septic tanks

Until the steam subsides,
And their bodies are matted with the wetness of leeches

Condom puppet shows,
Shiny billboards—
Vultures still nest in the city

Soot sky, lint of night in the village,
Ashen moon, crow-feathered masks,
Black spiral braids,
Djembe drummers and wailing

For children quiet as dolls
Stone eyes on the sidewalk
Carried across the sunset
On the camels of Mogadishu

They've stopped slicing up Mama
But left her body convulsing,
And our revolt?

Flinging dirt or laced letters
At vanishing ships

MOSQUITO-NET RHAPSODY

I left the steel pans in the rain
Huddling under plastic shawls

Drunk steel wool collapses under sudsy stars,
You left the kitchen light on

"Turn it off for me darlin"
I do

A Castries night, green bananas and lights on hills
Chasing each other every half hour

Palm trees glad to scrub their thick green hair
And brown slender bodies, I think of you.
Over green figs and ackee...

"Darlin, bring some water for me"
I do

Entering the bedroom with a cup almost glass,

"We don't have no ice"

You're beautiful—hair like steel wool still staggering,
Skin that's smooth as Mauby wrapped in silks,

Shutters fly open

"*Chuh*—leave dem"

Here we are,
Camped by the giant stone walls of Jericho,
Under a tent of nets, fortress of wind

I could sleep but the lights are bright,
Flashing, as the ghost ships come to moor,
Sinking the Pitons

"It's windy tonight"

Woe, woe unto you Jericho,
Tonight our brave storms pound your walls once more

Dawn,
Your walls fall,

Stabbed in the heart by palm trees

THE DREGS

gone are the nights
i used to resist
the voodoo of rum

my body, now a clear bottle
lifting sparkling breath
through the cove of country

asking you to come back,
from the steel fields,
from the gloomed city

to find me—
whisky squeezed from bananas,
under somebody's moon

SAY GOODBYE TO THE BEAUTIFUL VOICES

say goodbye to the beautiful voices
rhythm, tone, drum, jazz;
Old friend, say goodbye to
the beautiful ones

the days
when Mother moved as if possessed,
grown folk,
village, city
legs were drums, trees of oak,
with every strike earth would rise

throwing its head, hands to the future,
sokesodo,
up and down go the bones
and nothing has changed

fewer trees
lorries leave a'logging
money never comes back ...

old friend,
nothing has changed
but the beautiful voices are gone

I WILL BREAK THIS PEN

Shakespeare: dead on a cross
Eliot: spinning from a noose

We torch the schools, the libraries,
Civilians drag flaming busts through the streets
Breaking out eyes, chipping off lips

Imperialist heads tumble down the streets,
queens beaten out with brooms;
High heels flung back at the ambassadors

The ants come back to the hill
With pieces of the anteater

The trees resurrect to devour the lumberjack

Drums beat, pounding the body of Bach
Flutes play, tearing the clothes off Mozart

The griots pull the rug from under Greek mythology,
Let them tumble in the space of one Yoruba mind

They are fragments of the whole
The new shoot mocking the twilight of the plantain

We don't *need* to claim the pyramids
We don't *need* to lean on Timbuktu
There is rhythm in our step
There is art in our speech
Our children play with metaphysics in the sandbox

Let us snatch back our homes, our hearts, our minds

I will use my voice
I will break this pen

SKIN-BLEACHING CREAM

"You can sell a nigger anything,

Even leprosy"

HUNGER

How can we start the revolution,
When our poets litter the streets of Harlem?

When our freedom fighters are frail on hospice beds?
When our child prodigies cannot afford schooling?

Hunger:
It was as if I was pregnant with a demon,
Nestling near my intestines in a burning glow

And when I could, I wondered,
How can one man watch another man decay?

How can revolutionaries debate over wine and cheese
About africanizing the constitution
When the millions, the millions
With ideas, with working hands
Are left to dry under corrugated roofs
like salted meat?

There is intelligence in poverty
Brilliance in destitution

In the moment of hunger it was revealed to me:

Free the man; the man *is* the revolution

ALIENS

Ethiopian child, starving,
skin like the varnishing of bones,
guck in his eyelids,
attracting flies

hold his hand and take him to Times Square,
lead him naked to the centre
and let the pretty lights dance on his rib cage,
until his presence drives a wedge into the clockwork

and then you will find

all humans have a heart

WHEN THE FIRST DROPS FELL

when the first drops fell
I let them fall directly into my throat
wide-mouthed, pimpled with rain

I ran down to tell Bolivia
but he was already drenched, dancing
teeth like sugar cubes in his mouth

he pointed to Sri Lanka
who was transfixed,
watching a centipede flush back down
into a gutter

Mozambique's ululations were drowned
by the sounds of guns, hitting the floor,
as young girls caught floods in their skirts

Haiti was in such shock
she had to be ushered to the water—
assured that the shimmering puddles
were real diamonds

and I ran out to shout!
children with wire cars beamed out of the townships
splashing, crying for someone to thank—

and there was Mr. IMF

skewered to a wall
by a hunger-mad
ox

BAYAKOU

Hog slaughtered, dragged across glass shards
Sautéed in gutters, blood grunting in a pot,
Hen, crooked-eyed, peering through a hole in the slum
"Bayakou!" Rubbing down toilet bowls like a lover with oils,
Palms cupped to wells, drawing springs
As torches blaze through windows, house losing its footing,
Quaking, as she spills her salt and pushes out the zinc
To where even ribbed dogs snarl, and the hills writhe,
And the moon hisses and curls its light above her
As cockerels try to evacuate, tongues shrilling
Alarming the sun, she too shrivelled for pity, skin turned saltfish
Chafing against her fingers, she would sooner flush
This whole Cité, hear it drain through her good ear
While the wretched, the wrecked, ooze from collapsed metal
Unsheathed, poisoned by blowfish, risen from stupors
As parrots drop from the sky like rain
Watching dark night lift its skirts from an island
In seizure, welts cresting in the waves, scabbing,
Peeling into salted sea

BASS WILSON FARMHAND

Bass Wilson had a farmhand once, named Dambudzo,
Called simply Dam

Bass Wilson's farm in Nyanga was a legend,
Stretching far, far,
As far as Mozambique

It was well well tended well well,

tended to by workers,
work, work, working workers black with sweat.

Dam was one, Dam's son Kudakwashe,
Was one as well

With town a distance, Bass
Saw no fit need for schools,
A hospital.

On his farm?

For whom?

It was simply him, Mrs. Wilson, Waffles the Missus' poodle,
And four hundred workers working strong.

As such like most mornings
Kudakwashe argued with the aged Dam

"Pasi nekudzvinyirirwa, ngatisunungukei!"

And that meant—

"Let's get free!"

Dam's mock reply

"Rusununguko kutambura,
don't follow these boys, seizing farms"

and that was that.

Dam fetched the work backie

For Bass Wilson,
Having long noticed the change in Rhodesia,
Had instructed Dam to escort Mrs. Wilson to the store
Every morning

Dam drove to the main house for "Mrs. Bass Bass"
In the cold morning air,
As he did every six-thirty,
Setting off into freezing Nyanga day.

Mrs. Wilson in the driver's
Waffles in the passenger's
Dam, in the open back burring along the elevated slopes.

And having travelled in this manner for many a sleep,
Dam died (cough) (cough) slowly (cough) (cough)
of pneumonia (cough)

Kudakwashe,
Weeping,
by the unmarked grave of the father.

CAN YOU HEAR THE DRUMS?

Can you hear the drums? Can you hear the drums?

New York 1934
Record playing. Needle in static.
Dry martinis, marble counters and doubled-over spooks
Who understand their sorrow in the clink of drafts.
Mic skeletons. Ribs polished with red wine
As fedora hats begin to move towards the floor,
"Introducing to you, Lady Day"
Crack, Crack, Double-Barrel, Crack,
Broke the bartender into his glasses, twisted necks
And ran blood gushing like soda fizz.
No paramedics. A swaying chandelier flickering
As white hoods escape into the night. Dance.

Kingston 1996
Lizards run across a fence. A young boy crouches by the window
Hands filled with coconut water. Headlights blur around the corner.
Burnt spoons on cracked tiles.
The moon rises like she's spreading a tablecloth on cement walls
Preparing for the crash of Rasta skulls as they are frisked by police.
The headlights seem closer. The boy opens the window and slips out.
A slight rain startles the palm trees who look for their feet ready to
    "Skat!"

Walls break out in black freckles as bullets explode in the air,
Mimicking each ricochet. Jeeps swerve
As bodies bludgeon Zinc fences. Dance.

Soweto 1976
in translation ... Freedom! Freedom!
Shot. Shot. Shot. Shot. Shot.
Drop.
Heaps.

Can you hear the drums? Can you hear the drums?
The bongo thumping gainst the patter of bullets, dance
The bongo thumping gainst the patter of bullets, dance
Cuz when the Bongo thumps
it shatters the patters of bullets, dance
Cuz when the Bongo thumps
it shatters the patters of bullets, dance

for growing up poor in the projects,
sewing your clothes with your votes as you broke like the promise of
    politicians
Groping the smoke of your knowledge, smouldering cold cuz
    Europe was over-astonished and so they lit it tell me can you
    hear the drums?
Through suffering and tears
Can you hear the drums?
Send dust up in the air!

Can you hear the drums? Feel the rhythm while we locked in their
   prison listen to bongos sounding freedom Afrika move your
   feet and dance
Hear the drums, move your feet in the dust,
To cover our brothers up under their gutters erupting with
   hundreds of shots.

Can you hear the drums? Can you hear the drums?
Can you hear the drums? Can you hear the drums?
Can you hear the drums? Can you hear the drums?
Can you hear the drums? Can you hear the drums?
Can you hear the drums? Can you hear the drums?
Can you hear the drums? Can you hear the drums?

Dance, d-Dance, dance, Dance, d-Dance, dance, dance, dance ...

A–free–kah
A–free ...

OKAVANGO

antelope converse with stars
crocodiles at their ankles

hippos walk from one star-studded pool
and sink into the next,

zebras drink at the water's edge,
aardvarks serenade

whooping hyenas slobber,
ostrich run, attempt to fly,
lionesses fang into hides, blood on their chests

elephants trumpet, clouds imitate their form,
giraffes stalk the milky way,
nightbirds sing songs learned from echoes
of the zambezi

my hands dig into the warm body of the soil
clumps of God dusts out of my fingers

my religion is the spray of zimbabwe waterfalls,
my temple is the turquoise grasses,
i am anointed with peace

Okavango,
my soul runs to God

PECULIAR LIGHT

Dragonflies are like ...
Oil stains on water as the tide comes in around our ankles
Like a legion of small white ants,
Under the sway
Of trees
Our faces become leopard skin,
till stilled leaves leave us black.

Water on kinky hair is so much like the universe
The fading and the shooting stars every time we shake our fros,
It's here we reminisce,
Through cobwebs of constellations
Threading our hands as we make it to the view,
Peculiar light.

In peculiar light it's almost as if I've known you before,
Known your velvet skin, slim like the kettle steam, and me
Bubbling like a pot in Massa's kitchen
As you cut and diced his string beans,
I knocked at the window
Holding a garland of sweet corn to place atop your plaits,
But Massa saw,
And strung me up like those beans
Whipping me as you watched

Letting the North Star sink,
Down your cheek.

The network he left on my back
Seems as intricate as the multitude of men parqueting the slave-ship
    floor,
Where I lay shackled, indiscriminately,
Like hay in a haystack,
You shackled with me,
Though it seemed as if we were continents apart
Severed by darkness as the waves crashed between us,
And I imagined your face, with braids wrapped in sequence
You're beautiful, especially when the light hit you,
As Massa streaks his lantern cross the cargo of our people.

The two of us gripping wooden planks feels like …
When we use to lie on hills to feel the earth move between the stars,
    Alkebulan,
You traced the design of pyramids in the palm of my hand
Your velvet skin, slim in the moonlight,
Your locks lured me like a stubborn ox
Gusting breaths from nostrils breaking chains off the harness
Yet still I feared to step into your ocean,
As you rippled waves like tinsel
Your wading silhouette surreal before the rising sun
As the universe shakes her fro and leaves us black.

Where were we? We were where we were,
where the tide comes in,
And the dragonflies skim on the water,
In peculiar light.

THE SOJOURNERS

Flying fish
Darting from the blue moons of Haiti
To the stars of Oyo

Men grow fins on the coasts of Haiti
Diving into the sea
Trailing stars in the water
Darting through ghosts of the passage

"It is said our gods swam through these waters
Trailing beneath the slave-ships
In schools of fish

It is said when they harpooned squids for food
It was braided Ogun snagged in the net
Who sharpened our teeth with his fingernails

When bodies were heaved into the sea
Like rancid cornmeal
It is said that the hiss was not of bubbles

But of laughter

It is said when they rifled the first rebel
They found her heavy to drag—
On account of her cow legs

And then the empiricists began to sweat
As they fired at approaching slaves
And found locusts for gunpowder

And after blood sparked like red stars
And the empiricists were egg white on the beach
Erzulie walked to the clouds
Toussaint dead in her arms
Bleeding stars that ..."

                    lead to Oyo

Tonight
Under a blue moon
Flying fish dive off the coasts
Trailing stars
Arching through water

Tonight
We sojourners return

To Ile-Ife

KUMINA

krik
too many stories,
krak

the body of Son-Jara is dragged
borne on the back of his grieving Tarantula
to the brightest streetlight

Kumina
skirt-swirl of blue rain over blue mountains
tambourines of thunder
storm clouds, creolizing the night sky

and we pay tribute

to those in the fields
who were ready to hack artwork
into white skulls

crouched in the bushes
while macca waited with them in ambush
with pine-prickles of guerrilla warfare

and "oyinbo he deh come"

and they suffocated him
smothered him
smothered him till our hands were wet with sweetsop

krik
i said, too many stories,
krak

Guinea-man you walk
pregnant with ill-charted constellations
leaving pellets of stars, horns pointing to closer moons

Guinea-man, Guinea-man

what am I to do with these
when my poetry tastes like salt, and I am unable to fly?

Guinea-man.

they ran, trekked
up mountains sour to sable feet, bitter like rind
leaves and grass no longer docile,
dancing, spinning, spirals of wet skin, vibrant, bursting with oxygen

Guinea-man.

my stories swim around my black skin
they're too heavy for me, weighing me down
like a donkey pulling a wheel-less cart

i stall

in somebody's field
contemplating from the observatory of tall grass
the Diaspora of stars

In turquoise sea,
the Kra of the millions thrown overboard
await the ceremonial trail,
as Son-Jara is dragged under streetlights
back to the ocean's coast,
Anansi spinning His web
over the passage

Guinea-man, I wan go home.

let me join this procession of stars
constellations charted with spider's silk
silver threads shining over ocean salt

I cannot fly
But I will crawl.

GLOSSARY

Ackee yellow fruit, part of Jamaica's national dish, ackee and saltfish

Africville century-old black community in Nova Scotia bulldozed by the Canadian government

Afrikan spelling Africa with a *k* symbolizes an Afro-centric/Pan-Afrikan worldview

Albion Mall shopping mall in Rexdale, Toronto, frequented by immigrants

Alkebulan Afrika

Anansi spider, trickster deity (West Afrika/Caribbean)

August Town a "depressed" community in Jamaica

Ba bird ancient Kemetic soul bird

Babymother the unwed mother of one's child

Backie pickup truck (Southern Africa)

Bagga/Baggaman Bagmen, the homeless

Basmati basmati rice, a type of rice grown in India

Bass extremely servile way of saying "Boss"

Bayakou in Haiti, a person who goes door to door to collect human waste

Blue-bins Toronto recycling bins

Boillion French-Caribbean dish, a soup containing different meats

Boogo boogo a Jamaican word imitating the sounds of heavy bass in music

Bully Beef corned beef (Jamaican)

Bunx bounce against (West Indian)

Bust break/burst

Bwoy boy

Callaloo green leafy vegetable similar to spinach

Canada/Canadian a lowercase c in Canada/Canadian signifies
a rejection of State Canada's rhetoric, which attempts to
represent Canada as a free and democratic state, and the
recognition of Canada's existence as a settler colony and
project of European imperialism and white supreamacy

Canuck Canadian

Castries capital of St. Lucia

Chibuku an alcoholic drink, often home-brewed, made from
fermenting sorghum (millet); "shake-shake" is slang for
chibuku

Chobe, Sedudu beautiful wildlife reserve in Botswana

Chuh expression of frustration (Jamaican)

Cipher group of people gathered to debate or freestyle (rap)

Cité Cité Soleil, the largest slum in Haiti

Did deh to be around/to be there

Djembe West Afrikan drum

Don't it? "Isn't that right?" (Jamaican)

Dung down

Dutch pots large steel pots used in Jamaica

Erzulie Haitian goddess of love

Everything is everything life goes on even through tribulation

Fiend to act like a crack addict

fro Afro

Ghibo exclamation

GO Station Ontario's interregional transit system

Green figs part of St. Lucia's national dish, green fig and saltfish

Griots West Afrikan storytellers

Gwaan Go on (Jamaican)

Halifax large regional municipality in Nova Scotia

Hardo Bread a Jamaican bread

Ile-Ife sacred place of creation for ancient Yoruba people/founding city of the Yoruba

Inshallah "God willing"

JAH God (Rastafarian)

Jambalaya Creole food; a rice dish

Jane and Finch "depressed" community in Toronto, heavily populated with Jamaican immigrants

Jumping the broom Afrikan-American marriage tradition

Just like magnet to steel from Jah Cure's "Longing For": "Just like magnet to steel, your love keeps pulling me in"

Kente cloth traditional Ghanaian cloth

Kra soul, life force, destiny, piece of God (West Indian, Akan)

Krik? Krak! traditional opening of Creole story in French Caribbean

Kumina Jamaican traditional dance and religion

Kwaito popular South African music and culture (similar to African-American hip-hop in its cultural impact among black South African youth)

"Laku Tshoni 'Ilanga" love song by famous South African singer

Miriam Makeba

Ma kwere kwere foreigner (first used as name for refugees)

Macca prickly bush (Jamaican)

Manicous opossum (Trinidadian)

Maroons slaves that escaped and often fought slave masters through guerrilla warfare; some were sent to Nova Scotia in 1796, then on to Sierra Leone in 1800

Mas playing Mas; jumping up in a costume at carnival

Massa master

The Matrix American sci-fi movie

Mauby dark drink made from Mauby bark (Eastern Caribbean)

Me head a gadda wata Jamaican expression meaning "I am becoming forgetful/senseless"

Mi deh yah "I'm here" (Jamaican)

Mopane Botswana delicacy

Mosquito-net large net attached to the ceiling and spread over the bed to keep mosquitoes out

Naps/nappy *see* peppercorn head

Ndoko the Ngbandi say the heartbeat (Ndoko) is a water bird bobbing in and out of water

Nyanga an expansive farmland area in Zimbabwe

Obeah West Indian magical arts

Ogun Yoruba god of war

Oxtail the skinned tail of an ox, used in Jamaican cuisine

Oyinbo white man (Yoruba)

Oyo ancient Yoruba kingdom

Pacino Al Pacino, American actor famous for gangster roles

Pap ground millet, similar to rice in its role as a staple food

Peenie-wallie fireflies (Jamaican)

Peppercorn head rolls of short, sparse, kinky hair (also "naps"/ "nappy head")

Pitons twin coastal peaks off the coast of St. Lucia that look like mountains that have broken through the surface of the sea

Poco Pocomania religion; at church the women wear white dresses and hair wraps

Rahtid mild expletive (Jamaican)

Red light, green light a childhood game; one must walk or run when the leader calls "green light" and freeze when he/she calls "red light"

Regent Park publicly funded housing project in Toronto

Rice and peas Jamaican cuisine

Riddim rhythm, also the instrumental music in a reggae song

Round yah around here

Run a team

Salif Keita famous Malian tenor

Saltfish salted codfish

San a people of Botswana, masters of archery

Secretary bird large long-legged bird that kills snakes with its feet

Seswaa pounded/shredded meat, Botswana cuisine

Schooler a uniformed elementary school student (Jamaican)

Scotians Nova Scotians

Shake-Shake *see* Chibuku

Shebeen Southern African drinking spot (especially an illegal one)

Silk cotton tree sacred tree of Afrikans of the Diaspora and West Afrika

Sokesodo up and down

Son-Jara Sundiata, main character of West Afrikan Epic

Spook derogatory term for Afrikans

Steel pans Eastern Caribbean musical instrument

Stock sweets candy

Sun hot hot sun (Jamaican)

Sweetsop sweet, green fruit

Thabo common name in Southern Africa

Thebe Botswana money (coin)

Times Square famous landmark in New York City

Toussaint Haitian revolution leader

Trodding a Rastaman's walk through Babylon (the worldly system)

Tswana a people of Botswana; majority of the population

TTC Toronto Transit Commission; public transportation system (bus, subway, et cetera)

Tuck shop a convenience stand that sells food, candy, et cetera

Warner women Jamaican seers

Yemoja Yoruba goddess of the ocean. Also "Yemaya"/"Yemaja" (Cuban)

ABOUT THE AUTHORS

YANNICK MARSHALL

Yannick Marshall is a young Afrikan poet of St. Lucian and Jamaican heritage. He has spent much of his life in the community of Rexdale in Toronto, Canada, a community heavily populated with Jamaican, West African, and Sri Lankan immigrants. He has also lived in Jamaica, St. Lucia, and Botswana. He is currently studying Political Science, Caribbean Studies, and English at the University of Toronto and at the University of the West Indies. His poems have been published in *Kola Magazine*, the *T-Dot Griots Anthology*, Ishmael Reed's *Konch Magazine*, and *Wasafiri*.

YEMI AGANGA

Yemi Aganga is a young Afrikan poet of Nigerian heritage and a citizen of Botswana. He has spent segments of his life in both Botswana and the United States and currently resides in Lesotho, where he is studying law at the National University of Lesotho. His poems have been published in *English in Africa Journal*, *Inkblots Magazine*, and Ishmael Reed's *Konch Magazine*.